MW01028287

# Dear Universe

# Dear Universe

LETTERS OF AFFIRMATION AND EMPOWERMENT

— FOR ALL OF US —

By
*Yolo Akili*

Micheal Todd Books | New York, NY

Dear Universe: Letters of Affirmation and Empowerment for All of Us

© 2013 Yolo Akili Robinson

All rights reserved.
No part of this book may be reproduced in any form or by any means, electronic or mechanical, including photocopying, recording, or by any other information storage and retrieval system or technologies now known or later developed, without permission in writing from the publisher.

Edited by Phyllis Alesia Perry and Lisa C. Moore
Cover and book design by Eunice Corbin

ISBN: 978-0-615-77214-1

Printed in the United States of America

# FOREWORD

Few moments in life are as significant as the moment when we awaken to Self – that is, the moment when we realize that we are Divine, not just bones and flesh, roles and labels, titles and possessions. The recognition of our own Innate Divinity, the Indwelling Spirit, is the moment when we truly ascend to humanness and begin to realize its glorious and astounding potentials. It is the moment when the mysteries of the Universe begin to unfold to us personally and miracles are no longer merely theoretical. We stop relying on handed-down wisdom and start listening to the Inner Voice. This is also the moment when we begin to discern the Innate Divinity in others. It is the beginning of peace on Earth, wisdom and illumination. It is also a moment of profound Love.

My former student and much-beloved friend Yolo Akili has assembled a series of insights, life lessons, and affirmations that guide all of us toward recognition and expression of our Innate Divinity. By reminding us that even our imperfections are Divine, he eases us into the relaxation necessary to begin affirming ourselves in ways that society often doesn't. His wise insights help us to see behind the veil created by our anxieties, fears, angers, jealousies and doubts. But Yolo doesn't stop here, and this is where his offerings really expand the world of inspirational and self-help writings: He incorporates a finely tuned social justice orientation that incorporates and puts a new twist on the insights we often associate with critical theory and liberation movements. To bring the two together is truly Yolo's gift to all of us.

*Dear Universe* helps us see that when we encounter and embrace the truth of who we are, we become empowered to use that truth to benefit all humanity; indeed, all creation. As Yolo writes, "Your story can help save someone's life." Take this to heart! There is nothing to be afraid or ashamed of; our imperfections and dark corners are part of our perfection and Light. We must embrace the paradox that, at the same time our agency is nearly limitless, systems that work vigorously to negate and dehumanize us also exist. We must learn to see – really see – Self and systems of oppression (both of which tend to be hidden from us in ordinary life), and learn to use Self to transform and transcend such systems – until not only are we ourselves transformed, but so is all humanity and life on Earth. What Yolo's love-filled and inviting text reminds us is that, when we awaken from self to Self, things shift in the Universe. In fact, shifting from self to Self is perhaps the most profound and liberating political act.

Layli Maparyan
August 26, 2012
Wellesley, MA

# Introduction

*What exactly is the Universe?*

Well, the answer to that question would depend on whom you ask. To some, the Universe is a ball of quantum particles, randomly reconstructing reality at whim. To some, the Universe is a living-breathing creature, a conscious entity that intertwines with and touches us in every aspect of our lives.

As far as I'm concerned, the Universe is you. And your mother. And your cousin Pookie. Uncle Harold and Aunt Minnie. Not to mention Ms. Oswald, your third-grade teacher, who used to pop you on the wrist with a ruler. Yep, her too. All of them are the Universe. All of them are a part of this cosmic whatchamacallit, this great collective life experience that we each are engaging in. And you know what? Each of us is an important part of this Universe.

Now I know you may find that hard to believe, but even scientific research supports this. Science says all life is energy and energy can never be created or destroyed; it can only be transformed. So the only logical conclusion I can come to, based on that premise, is that you can't be created (at least not again) or destroyed.

In some way you are always going to be here. That means that you are not only needed in this moment, but you are needed and necessary in all moments. You are an inalienable absolute in all life. We will always have you!

So this book is a message from the Universe to you from me. And yes your mama. And cousin Pookie. And Uncle Harold. It's a conglomeration (that's a fancy word for collection) of affirmations, prayers, praises and gifts that we are giving to you to help you remember your greatness. 'Cause sometimes you forget! And you being a big part of life that can never be created or destroyed, well, we all need you to remember! We need you to know that you have a purpose! We need you to know that you are loved! That way you can go about your way spreading more love to other people just by being your beautiful, fabulous self!

You can flip through this book any time, day or night, and find a little piece of that love, a little bit of inspiration to keep you going. A little bit of fuel to get you back on the right path. This is my gift to you.

It's not designed with any religion in mind. It's designed with Spirit in mind. And Spirit is just love. Love for all of creation. Love for the foolishness and the funk, love for the joy and the sorrow, love for the opportunities for tomorrow. It's all in here.

This book means a lot to me. 'Cause I wrote it (with the help of Pookie and Uncle Harold, of course) at a time when I really needed some inspiration; at a time when I really needed to remember who I was and what magic I, and the people around me, were capable of. I trust that this tiny book will do the same for you.

I trust and hope that it will empower not only you but your community. I trust and hope it will help you empower your family—help you all empower each other. Empower each other to love harder. Empower each other to trust the voice within. Empower each other to change the world without. Empower each other to remember: You are the Universe. So how can you ever have an excuse for not being great?

*With love always,*
*Yolo*

# Acknowledgements

*To the Universe, thank you for allowing me to be a channel for the creation of this book. Thank you for sparking the idea and giving me the energy to bring it into fruition. Thank you for trusting me.*

*To my mother and father Michael and Patricia Robinson, thank you for providing me with the love that allowed me to grow. Thank you to my grandmother, Lottie Cuyler, for nurturing that love through Spirit. Thank you to my sister, Patrice Robinson, and my brother, Marcus Robinson, for being such wonderful reasons to love. Thank you to my friends, constellations in arms, for encouraging me to create by shining so brightly on your own: Moya Bailey, Kenyon Farrow, Tamara Jones, Nicole Cain, Nathan Yungerberg, Tina Martin, Mia Mingus, Stacy Lafay White, Samietra Lisenbee and many, many more. A very special gratitude to Seitu Jemel Hart, a sun in his own right, for sharing and supporting this process with me. Thank you Layli, for offering your magic and words to this book through the foreword. I am truly honored. Thank you to Phyllis Alesia Perry for nurturing the vision.. Thanks to Eunice Corbin and Lisa Moore for your creative brilliance. Thank you to all the people who have supported me throughout the years. I hope that this tiny book means as much to you as it does to me.*

*With love always,*
*Yolo*

*May this book be used as a tool to help transform trauma....*
*and lead us all to recognize the love we already are.*

# Dear Universe

Dear Universe,

Today I ask that you help me to realize: *the world does not need my perfection – it needs my **truth.***

**BREAKING NEWS:** The Universe is not waiting for you to get it all together.

**THIS JUST IN:** The Universe secretly knows that you (and nobody else for that matter) has ever had it all together.

**NEWS FLASH:** The Universe knows a lot of y'all been running 'round here trying to act like you do have it all together. The Universe also knows that some of y'all been waiting on everything to come together before you get started on what you really desire for your life.

**FRONT PAGE HEADLINE:** The Universe is currently seeking those who don't "have it together." The Universe is seeking radically imperfect, eccentrically inaccurate individuals to share their improper and illuminating art, skills, talent and truth with the world.

Apply. Within. *You.*

*Universe, today I do not let my quest for perfection prevent me from sharing my light.*

Dear Universe,

Today I ask that you help me to understand: *Only my inner compass can lead me to my outer destiny.*

There is an internal piece of us that always knows which way to go. It sends us signals through our body. It sends us messages in our surroundings.

Many of us have been taught not to trust this inner guiding force. We have been taught that tangible proof always trumps our intangible feelings. We have been taught that our feelings are far less powerful than the intellectual mind. Yet in order for us to reclaim our inner power, we must recognize and relive all the times in which our inner compass pointed us in a direction and we didn't follow it. What was the consequence? Where did we end up?

Now ask yourself: Do you really want to be back there again, with that aching voice in your gut saying, "I told you so"?

*Universe, today I ask that you help me to follow my inner compass.*

**From the PR DEPARTMENT OF THE UNIVERSE:**

**FOR IMMEDIATE RELEASE**

**S.I.N. = Self-Inflicted Nonsense.** You were not born, nor are you presently, of evil or wrongdoing. You were born into circumstances, situations, systems and societies which hold ideas and beliefs. These forces converged to create a reality for the people who brought you here. What they taught you and how they treated you because of those ideas and systems is not a reflection of you, but of these forces. Anything painful that happened to you is not a reflection of your worth; it is only a commentary on how this world, because of these forces, has neglected your beauty and value as a human being.

*Don't let their neglect become your own.*

Dear Universe,

Today I ask that you help me to *liberate myself from the imaginary monsters I have made up in my mind.*

Many of us live Scooby-Doo lives. We run, panicked, around large empty haunted houses (our minds), chased by imaginary, made-up monsters (our fears).

Like Scooby and the gang, when we confront these monsters and unmask them, we often find out they're not as scary as we thought. In fact, we often find out the monsters are not even *real.*

Today, I want to invite you to be like Scooby and the gang. Set a trap for those goblins and ghouls you have in your head. Once you catch them, unmask them and take a good, hard look at what they really are underneath all the face paint, rubber masks and makeup. They may not be quite as scary as you think. In fact, they may end up looking a lot like **you**.

*Universe, today help me to unmask my internal monsters and see them for the irrational fears they are.*

**A Message from the Universe:**

*Remember:* Oppression thrives off isolation. Connection is the only thing that can save you.

*Remember:* Oppression thrives on superficiality. Honesty about your struggles is the key to your liberation.

*Remember:* Your story can help save someone's life. Your silence contributes to someone else's struggle. Speak so we all can be free. Love so we all can be liberated. The moment is now. *We need you.*

Dear Universe,

Today I ask that you help me to remember: *I am essential to the structure of existence itself.*

SPIRITUAL PRINCIPLES OF LIFE:

1. Energy cannot be created nor destroyed; it can only be transformed.

2. The essence of you, the intangible entity that inhabits and colors the physical container you embody, is energy.

3. Because who you are is energy, you have always existed and will always exist in some shape or form. Your essence will recycle, transmute and transform for millennia to come, expressing different states of consciousness and being.

4. Because you are here, and always have been, you must understand: You are an integral part of reality. The Universe is consciousness; the Universe is life itself. We are all cells in the body of the Universe. We are a part of this greater organism, unfathomable to the waking human imagination.

5. Your purpose in this lifetime plays an important role in the ever-evolving schemata that we call "life." As life grows and changes, after this world ends and when another one begins, you will still be. You are a part of everything that is. You have a role to carry out. As humans, as life, as Spirit, we need you.

Remember this when they tell you that you don't belong.

Remember this when they tell you that who you are is "wrong."

Remember this when they try to silence you, erase you, belittle you or betray you.

Remember and tell them this:

You cannot erase me, because I am essential to the structure of existence itself. It is only because I am *that you can even be*. The Spirit that animates me with life is a testimony from the Universe to my worthiness. It is the symbol that has marked my being as sacred. You can attempt to destroy this form I inhabit, but the essence of what I am will always exist. You can attempt to purge me from your vision, but your consciousness will always conjure me. In this lifetime, as in all others, despite your petty prejudices or socially structured stigmas, I am yours and you are mine. We are each other's, and locked in this immortal erotic dance of life, we will always be.

*Universe, today I affirm that I am an essential aspect of an extraordinary universe.*

Dear Universe,

Today I ask that you help me to understand: *Provocation is a concept affirmed by people who do not know their power.*

Provocation is based on the idea that someone can make you do something. It is based on the idea that you have so little self-control that you can be a puppet. It is based on the idea that you have no control over your own tongue and body.

The reality is someone can do something that will awaken an intense feeling within you. Someone can call you a name and it can awaken a feeling of anger within you. Someone can take an action and it can awaken a feeling of jealousy within you.

However, what you choose to do with that feeling that is awakened within you is your choice. No one can take your hand and make you hit someone. No one can take your tongue and make you speak harshly. As a human being and as an adult, the choices you make about what to do with your body in response to others' words and actions are ultimately yours and yours alone.

*Universe, today I remember: When I have self-control, I have the power.*

YOLO AKILI

Dear Universe,

Today I ask that you help me to remember: *Unexpressed anger is violence against the self.*

Unexpressed anger will hurt your body and your spirit. Unexpressed anger will clog your veins and upset your stomach. Unexpressed anger will keep you up at night and keep you away from those that you love.

Most of us know this. Still, some of us hold on to the anger. We hold on to it because we have been told that being angry is not nice. We have been told that "sucking it up" is the appropriate thing to do. Yet when we do "suck up" our emotions, we end up living the consequences. We suffer because that anger will show up somewhere else. Our unexpressed rage at a partner may show up against the kids. Our unexpressed rage at a job may show up against our parents. Our unexpressed rage at ourselves will often show up in our bodies.

For the sake of your self and your community, find a way to express your anger. Express your anger in a way that will heal instead of hurt. Express your anger in a manner that will propel you toward understanding and *not perpetuate cycles of harm.*

Express that anger in a way that gets it off your chest and out of your aura. 'Cause the more you let that anger go, the more room you have inside to let love *in.*

*Universe, today I am honest about being angry.*

## A MESSAGE FROM THE UNIVERSE:

Stop struggling: Be still.
Stop pouting: Be peace.
Stop whining: Be grateful.
Stop rushing: Be patient.
Stop looking: Be present.

The answer is within you.

Dear Universe,

Today I ask that you help me to understand: *What I think about the group of people I belong to, I unconsciously think of myself.*

**NEWS FLASH:** If you are gay, and think that all gay people are manipulative, superficial and can't be trusted, then that means you think that you are manipulative, superficial and can't be trusted.

**THIS JUST IN:** If you are a black person and think that black people are triflin', deceitful and unprofessional, then this means that you think that you are triflin', deceitful and unprofessional.

**BREAKING NEWS:** You are a reflection of the identity groups you belong to. You are a reflection of those identity groups that you do not belong to. You are a reflection of human life. Any exaggerated and stereotyped ideas you have about a group of humans reflects unexamined exaggerated ignorance you have within you.

*Universe, today I ask for the strength to eliminate the prejudice-ridden, preconceived ideas in my heart and mind.*

Dear Universe,

Today I ask that you help me to remember: *Scarcity is not the natural state of the universe.*

There is enough food. *The problem is we live in a system that does not support everyone being fed.*

There is enough water. *The problem is we live in a system that does not quench the world's thirst.*

There is enough shelter. *The problem is we live in a system that does not put a roof over everyone's head.*

Fact:

Less than 1 percent of the world's population *captures more than 39 percent of the world's wealth.* *

So is the problem that there is not enough? Or is the problem that we are not using what we have wisely?

*Universe, today I ask that you help me recognize how I contribute to a culture of scarcity in my own life and in the world.*

*Statistic from:* Shaping a New Tomorrow: How to Capitalize on the Momentum of Change, The Boston Consulting Group, May 2011.

## A MESSAGE FROM THE UNIVERSE:

Be humble.

Or be *humbled.*

Dear Universe,

Today I ask that you help me to remember: What may seem like a setback today may actually be the Universe *aligning forces for what I will need tomorrow.*

A message:

Sometimes things have not happened because circumstances have not aligned for them to *prosper.*

Sometimes things have not happened because you are not properly equipped to *persevere.*

Sometimes things have not happened because the potential for failure is too *pervasive.*

And sometimes things have not happened because you have some *healing* to do in order to herald them into your life.

It's important to remember:

The world does not operate on your ego's timeline. Things will come into being when they are needed, when they are necessary, and when each of us has done the work to be ready.

*Universe, today I remember: When and if I am ready, what I desire will come to pass.*

Dear Universe,

Today help me to remember that jealousy is a *lack of fulfillment*.

Jealousy is a *signal*. It is a signal that you do not understand that you are an authentic, unprecedented expression of the Divine. It is a signal that you do not understand that the traits, power and potential you possess cannot be replicated or renounced. It is a signal that you are seeking external validation for that which you can only find within.

The next time you feel jealous, take a moment to check yourself. Are you devaluing how amazing you are? Downplaying the awesome things that you have done by comparing yourself to others?

If you find this to be true, be still. Breathe deeply and redirect your energy. Remember: *Comparison is a tool used by those with a lack of imagination who do not respect Divine order.*

Now show some respect to the Universe. Create fulfillment in your own life. And stop acting like you aren't an original.

*Universe, today I realize that when I am fulfilled, I am not jealous.*

Dear Universe,

Today I ask that you grant me the courage to be disciplined.

Help me stay "in the now" even as I *plan for the future.*

Help me to pace with *patience.*

Help me to plan with *intent.*

Help me to give thanks for the *work that will come* (and what went).

Help me to complete all the projects that *I have begun.*

Help me to sharpen all the projects that *I will begin.*

Help me to improvise when those plans *don't fall into place.*

Help me to forgive when I or someone else makes *mistakes.*

Help me create work that *heals, nourishes and feeds*
my soul, my mind and my wallet.

Please!
*And so it is!*

*Universe, today I practice discipline in my work.*

Dear Universe,

Today I ask that you help me to remember that sometimes *when I feel it that is all the proof that I need.*

It looks good. It sounds good. But you don't feel good about it. Even though all the ducks are lined in a row. Even though all the packages are neatly wrapped. Something still doesn't feel right about it, does it? And let me guess, you aren't going to say anything because other than that aching feeling in your gut, you think you don't have any proof.

Well, I am here to tell you: *That aching feeling in your gut is all the proof that you need!*

That feeling in your gut means something is awry. That feeling in your gut means something might be "off." That feeling is Spirit directing you to take a seat or step back before some foolishness shows up on your doorstep! That feeling is your Spirit's way of sounding the alarm that all may not be what it seems!

So don't ignore it! Don't just roll over or pull the sheets over your head! The next time that alarm goes off you better check the clock and figure out what time it is!

*Universe, today I realize my gut feelings are the alarms that let me know when foolishness is afoot.*

Dear Universe,

*Today it ends.*

Today fear will no longer limit my choices. Today fear will no longer restrict my possibilities. Today fear will no longer chart my path.

Today I am confronting fear head-on. I am *taking my life back*. I am taking my joy back. Today, fear, you and me are going head-to-head and just in case you didn't know, the entire *Universe* has my back.

I will not be moved. I will not be shaken. I have what it takes to take you out of the equation, and I will not rest until my faith in myself is fully restored.

*Universe, today I end the reign of fear over my life.*

## A MESSAGE FROM THE UNIVERSE:

If you don't release it from your heart, it will continue to hurt you. The more emotions you don't express; the more pain you carry unshared; the more rage you swallow; the more those emotions will affect your body, your aura and your joy.

You have to find your outlets to release your emotions. Don't let the rage kill you. Don't let the sorrow stifle your Spirit. Don't let this world rob you of your light. We need you.

Dear Universe,

Today I ask that you help me realize: *Communication is about coming to an understanding, not about proving that my perspective is right.*

## PRINCIPLES OF HUMAN COMMUNICATION:

1. *Understand that you are not your ideas. You have ideas, but you are not the things that you think.* Understand this.

2. *Understand that "right" and "wrong" are not fixed concepts.* At some point in human history, it was "right" to beat your wife. At some point in human history, it was "right" to own slaves. The idea of right and wrong is always changing. And it will always vary from person to person. Your idea of "right" will not always be someone else's. Understand this.

3. *Understand decisions and consequences.* For every action, there are reactions. For every decision, there are consequences. Rather than labeling decisions as right and wrong, learn to talk specifically about the consequences. Getting clear about cause and effect will help you get clear about choice and direction. Understand this.

4. *Understand intent is not the same as impact.* Our decisions have an impact on others even when our intent is different. It is the consequences of that impact for which we must be accountable. Intending not to hurt someone does not erase or minimize the fact that you did. You must be accountable to that fact. Understand this.

5. *Understand that everyone interprets the world through their own ideas, past experiences, psychological framework, social location and pain.* You see the world based on where you have been. You see the world based on who you are, based on how you are perceived and how you perceive others. Those perceptions are not absolute. They are not the only truth, and they are not the only way of knowing things. Understand this.

6. *Understand understanding.* Understanding someone else means stretching beyond your viewpoint and version of reality. It means learning without judgment to be present with how someone else sees things. It means getting out of your own head. It does not mean giving up what you believe. It simply means listening to someone else's beliefs.

*Universe, today I communicate to create understanding, not to prove I am right.*

## A MESSAGE FROM THE UNIVERSE:

Create your own path.

Conjure your own rainbows.

Don't accept the continuum of colors canvassed before you as the only prisms of light possible. *There are more.*

Dear Universe,

*Help me to embrace the mess.*

Life is not all about the pretty. Life is also about the gunk, the junk and the funk. Life is about the squishy, squirmy things. Life is about the smelly, pungent things.

In order for us to live in balance, we need to accept that life will not always fall into our pretty mental boxes. We have to accept that sometimes life will spill over, and our mess will be all over the floor. When this happens, it's important to not rush out with our mops, working to clean it up before anyone else can see it. Instead, it is important to sit in it. Be present with it. Do not wallow in it; just examine it. Learn the texture of your mess. What does it smell like? What does it look like? Where did it come from? How did it get here? How does it reflect you? What can it teach you?

You see, when we spend so much time rushing to clean up our mess, we miss out on all the insight our messiness can teach us.

*Universe, today I am not afraid of my mess.*

Dear Universe,

Today I ask that you *prevent me from projecting the parts of myself I don't like.*

When we don't like certain qualities or traits, we often are unable to see them within ourselves. When we are not able to see them in ourselves, we project them onto other people. When we project them onto other people, we claim we "cannot understand them."

When we cannot understand "them" it is because we do not understand ourselves.

When we take the time to understand ourselves, we realize that we express all human traits at different degrees. Sure, we may not know what it is like to kill someone, but we know what it is like to be so consumed with rage that hurting someone becomes possible. The commonality lies not in the extremity of the act, but in the feeling. All of us experience emotions. We may have different ways of interpreting those emotions, but in each of us the core of what they are is the same.

*Universe, today I realize nothing human is unknown to me.*

Dear Universe,

Today I ask that you help me to understand: *I couldn't have done it differently because I didn't know how.*

Look back on your life. Look back on the choices you made. With some of those choices you thought, in that deciding moment, of doing something different. You explored other options and possibilities.

But you chose your choice.

And your choice had consequences. Those consequences had an impact on other people, sometimes in ways you didn't even understand or expect. Sometimes in ways that made you feel ashamed or embarrassed.

But you know what? You couldn't have done anything differently. If you could have, you would have. And you know what else? You can't go back and change those things now. It's not possible. The past has passed. The present has come. You cannot liberate yourself from the consequences of your choices yesterday by beating yourself up about them today. Look for the lesson. Record it in your heart, and step into this moment equipped, energized and able to make this moment new.

*Universe, today I realize that what I did has been done, and now it's up to me to do differently.*

Dear Universe,

Help me to remember *if the present looks like the past, it may mean I didn't learn the lesson.*

That person you are dating – do they seem familiar? Do they seem to do things the way that other person you dated did – that other person who got on your nerves and caused you pain?

That job you are working – does it feel like you've worked there before? Does the frustration your boss causes you remind you of that last not-so-pleasant boss? Does that nauseous feeling you get when you are walking in that door trigger memories of a past employment?

If you answer "yes" to any of these questions, you may need to re-enroll in a course in the school of life.

Now don't get in a huff; everybody has to repeat a course sometimes. In fact, the most successful people often repeat a course several times before they get it right.

How else do you think that they become *head of the class?*

*Universe, today I will repeat this course until I get it right.*

Dear Universe,

Today I ask that you help me realize *I have to give people back their own crazy!*

Watch out! Duck! Jump! All across the world, people are trying to give you their crazy! All across the world, people are trying to make their issues yours. Look out!

If you're not careful, the next thing you know you will be taking responsibility for someone else's choices. If you aren't cautious, the next thing you know you will start believing someone else's actions are about you.

You have to be careful! Crazy is everywhere and it's trying to come get you!

How do you avoid this horrible, yet widespread, phenomenon?

Simple. You've got to give people back their own crazy! You have to recognize that other people's choices are not a reflection of you. You have to let them know that their crazy is a reflection of them. And you have to know what your own crazy looks like, so you don't get it mixed up with someone else's!

*Universe, today I own my crazy, and give everyone else back theirs.*

Dear Universe,

Today I ask that you help me to realize: *I have never done it alone.*

Whatever it is, you never do it in isolation. There are always the ancestors and the imprints they left upon you. Their voices sustain you, nourish you and guide you. Their experiences teach you, lead you and inform you. They are a part of the internal voice you hear in your head that warns you away from danger. They are a part of that gut feeling you get when you are going in a challenging direction. They are faces, voices and energies – great-grandparents whom you look like, but never knew; ancient cousins who once wore your face.

Wherever you are in life, they walk with you. The sooner you recognize this, the sooner you can stop believing you are doing it all alone. You can stop believing that it is all up to you. You have a role, but your role is carried on many unseen shoulders and built upon many unseen works. Do not ignore this. Ask for their assistance. Trust their guidance. And don't ever be fooled into thinking you are on your own.

*Universe, today I remember: Wherever Spirit is, I am always in good company.*

## A MESSAGE FROM THE UNIVERSE:

You know that thing you don't want to do? That thing that infuriates you? That thing that gets on your nerves? That thing to which you turn your nose up?

Yeah ... *that thing.*

Take a moment with me and just ponder: What if that thing had something to offer you? What if it had something to teach you? What if that thing, despite how crazy it looks, despite how demented it seems, really had a gold nugget buried deep inside?

What if that experience could lend you a skill or a tool that could help you in ways that you've never imagined? What if it could help you learn something new about who you are or what your purpose is in life?

Guess you'll never know, huh? Unless ... of course... you do that thing.

*Universe, today I understand that sometimes the things that I don't want to do have something valuable to teach me.*

Dear Universe,

Today I ask that you help me to understand that *sometimes things must be broken down in order to be rebuilt.*

A poem:
Governments fall. Bank accounts deplete.
Cars break down.
Computers
become
obsolete.
Policies expire
and wounds heal.
If you spend your time complaining
the opportunity
stays concealed.

In every ending
our imagination offers a chance
but if we refuse to dream bigger
we remain imprisoned,
*entranced*
in social structures
that have served their purpose and died
yet fear keeps us
wishing them back;
be revived.

Dear Universe,

Today I ask that you help me to remember that my life is not a problem to be fixed; it is *a journey to be experienced.*

Don't be so busy trying to fix things that you can't stop on the side of the road of life to have some fun. Don't be so busy trying to fix your life. Don't be so busy trying to fix you. Don't be so busy trying to fix your grandma, your daddy, your partner or your boss that you miss out on the reality that life is not about fixin'!

Life is about living the experience. Smelling the roses. Tasting the vegetables. Sipping the mimosa! Life is about the journey. Life is about luxuriating in the good stuff, learning from the bad stuff, and having as much fun with all that stuff as you can!

*Universe, today I am living the journey.*

Dear Universe,

Today I ask that you help me *separate the narratives in my head from the realities in my life.*

Every day we tell ourselves stories about what we think is happening around us. We have complete mythical tales, full of daring heroes, evil villains and courageous crusades. These stories are often based on our own life histories. They are based on our own assumptions and what we believe about people – which is really an extension of what we believe about ourselves.

Even as these stories can be entertaining, they can also be a far cry from the truth. They can inhibit us from growing, or from seeing the world around us as it really is. They can help keep up a steady cycle of pain, lies and deceit. In order to stop the cycle, we have got to take a step back and look at the story we've been telling ourselves. We have to ask ourselves: Is it the complete truth? Is there another perspective that we are missing? Is this an old narrative we are recycling? And ask perhaps the most important question: "Why are we so committed to continuing this tired storyline?"

*Universe, today I realize the world in my head isn't always the world as it is.*

## A MESSAGE FROM THE UNIVERSE:

If your body was a separate person, would it like you? Would it feel you were wrong? Wrong for the mean things you say to it every day? Wrong for the things you feed it that dishonor its wellness? Wrong for the ways you ignore it?

Let's take an assessment. When was the last time you said something nice to your body?

When did you last say thank you to your heart for beating? When was the last time you said thank you to your skeleton for holding you together? When was the last time you said thank you for all the things your body does for you?

You see, your body doesn't ask for appreciation, but it works 24 hours a day, 365 days a year. It doesn't take coffee breaks. There are no unions or minimum wage requirements for its work. Yet still it keeps on working for you, trying its best, putting in overtime.

Considering all the work that your body does for you, you could spend more time celebrating its uniqueness, rather than comparing it to someone else's body. You could spend some time feeding it food worthy of a child of the Universe instead of junk. You could offer it some rest and relaxation. You could show it some love, and if nothing else you could just say **thank you**.

*Universe, today I thank my body for all it does for me.*

Dear Universe,

Today I ask that you help me to understand that healing isn't about a past wound going away; it's about having a relationship to a past wound *that will not hinder me in the present moment.*

Our wounds don't ever go away. They are always there in our hearts and in our minds.

The actions of others can awaken these wounds. Along with those wounds, others' actions can also awaken feelings of rage, hurt, despair or frustration. Those feelings, once awakened, can lead us to make unwise choices in the heat of the moment. Those choices can help to recreate the very situations we are trying to avoid.

This is how we let our wounds get in the way of living our lives.

It's only when we get clear about our wounds that we can prevent them from impairing our judgment. When we get clear about our wounds, we can catch ourselves from falling into past patterns or from telling the narratives that lead us to act aggressively. Getting clear about our wounds means recognizing the root of where they come from. It means seeing that those intense feelings we are experiencing are often connected to a past pain that we are reliving and bringing to the present moment.

It doesn't have to be this way. You see, every time a wound is awakened, there is an opportunity to heal. Every time that a feeling comes up, you can talk back to it. Every time that memory is triggered, you can work to heal it. You can work to heal it by retelling the story – this time without the blame, the shame or the guilt. You can work to heal it by changing the frame – no longer seeing yourself or someone else as "bad" or "good" but human. You can work to heal by forgiving those involved and yourself.

Remember: A wound can be a guiding post. A wound can give you a moment to pause, an opportunity to reflect. They only impede us when we ignore them, deny them or try to act like they will go away. The reality is they are always with us, and they can be used in service to us. They can be used as tools to transform the present and they can be used as tools to navigate the future.

*Universe, today I will not lose my way because of my wounds.*

Dear Universe,

Today I will remember: *Healing happens.*

Don't let the six o'clock news fool you with its ongoing tales of woe. Despite what you may be seeing on the news, or reading in the newspaper, somewhere, every moment of every day, healing is happening.

Even as you read this, someone somewhere is forgiving. At this very second, someone is choosing to not kill. Right this very instant, a community is being restored – a child is being protected, a racial injustice is being prevented, a tree is being planted, a garden being grown, a father and son are hugging, a cycle of trauma is being stopped, a church is changing a prejudiced position, a law is being passed protecting the innocent, a book is being written that will save a country, a mother and daughter are dancing, a baby is giggling, a homeless person is eating, a crisis is being diverted, a family is finding shelter, two women are finding love, and light is finding its way to a rainbow.

So don't let what you see on television confuse you. No matter what horrible things are happening, there are equally as many acts of healing happening at the same time.

*Universe, today I focus on the healing in the world.*

Dear Universe,

Today I ask that you help me remember that *just like people can be addicted to caffeine and sugar, some of us can become addicted to creating anxiety and stress.*

Do you like being stressed? Do you like being worn down and worn out?

What?

You say you don't? Well then, why do you keep inviting anxiety and stress into your life? Why do you keep on taking on more commitments than you can handle and more burdens than you can carry?

Why do you keep on saying yes when you need to say no, or saying nothing when you need to say stop?

Could it be that you are addicted to stress? Accustomed to anxiety? Could it be that you forgot you had another way that you could live? Could it be that you have forgotten peace? Forgotten calm? Could it be that you have neglected patience?

If this sounds like you, then you might be addicted to stress and anxiety! But wait – don't get stressed out about it (that would be counterintuitive). Get peace!

Start saying no to situations that create stress. Start saying yes to situations that create calm. Stop participating in the creation of anxiety in your life. Stop co-creating it, calling it into being or even considering it an option. Unhook yourself from the stress and anxiety IV, and get yourself a good cool glass of calm!

*Universe, today I enroll in stress and anxiety rehab.*

Dear Universe,

Today help me to remember: *Being "deep" is deeply problematic if that means I think I am better than anybody else.*

So you're deep, huh?

Mhmm.

You know stuff, don't you?

Mhmm. You have all those social theory books on the shelf, quotes from MLK, pictures of Gandhi and even a statue of Mother Teresa. Oooh, chile! Can't nobody tell you nothing, you so deep!

You are so deep that you don't see how you talk down to people who you don't think are as deep as you. So deep that you turn your nose up to people who don't see things the way you think they are, **'cause they ain't that deep.** So deep that no one wants to have a conversation with you. So deep that the room clears out when you open your mouth. So deep that the revolution had to D-list you because you were breaking up the meetings with all of your deepness!!!

So deep, that can't nobody come down into that hole in the ground to find you …

*Universe, today my deepness will not be my weakness.*

Dear Universe,

Today I am asking that you help me to realize: *"God" does not "favor" people.*

*God does not favor people. The Universe does not favor people.* It is a system of inequality that favors people. It is a system of inequality that creates injustice. It is a system made and maintained by humans, not some distant, cosmic being that we project out into the heavens.

You see, some people like to use God, Spirit or the Universe as a scapegoat for their own shortcomings. Some people like to use God, Spirit or the Universe as an excuse for what they haven't done. Some people like to use God, Spirit or the Universe as a way to evade accountability for what they have chosen.

The reality is it's the God in us that helps to keep inequitable systems going. It's the Universe in us that isn't doing something about injustice. It's the Spirit in us that needs to get up and make change. Any other God, Universe or Spirit ain't real, ain't gonna do nothing and, honestly, may be just a figment of your imagination.

*Universe, today I stop blaming an external God for the collective actions and choices that the God within each of us has made!*

Dear Universe,

Today I ask that you help me to understand: *Diversity is God.*

If we look at Earth, we can see a few things very clearly. There are millions of types of flowers, thousands of types of fruit, millions of kinds of insects. The most obvious and evident message creation around us conveys is: *Diversity is a part of life.* We can take this one step further, for if we define "life" as "God" then we can further understand that *diversity is God.*

We as humans often miss this. We spend our whole lives trying to make everybody else just like us. This is the basic source of human conflict. Instead of understanding that difference is an integral part of who we are, we fight for everyone to have the same religion, the same pattern of loving or the same cultural expression. Perhaps we should try to more effectively mirror creation around us. Instead of saying, "You are not like me and you are wrong 'cause you are not like me, and I must destroy/silence/belittle you," maybe we could say, "You are different from me. Now how can we live together with those differences in balance, love and equity?"

*Universe, today I reflect and embrace the diversity that is the Universe.*

Dear Universe,

Today I ask that you help me to remember to *stay in my own vibration.*

Everybody has a vibe. A frequency. A vibration. Some people vibrate quickly, some people vibrate slowly. Some people vibrate erratically, some people vibrate gently. Everyone's vibe is different.

And everyone's vibe impacts the vibes of others.

In fact, some people want you to vibrate like them! Some people want to bring you into their stress vibration, or their angry vibration. Some people want to force you into their happy vibration, or their joy vibration. All that pushing and shoving can totally throw you out of whack! That's why you must work to stay in your own vibe.

What does that mean? That means if you are having a good day, keep your good day vibes. If you are having a sad day and need to be sad, keep your sad day vibes. Every vibe is necessary. We only get into trouble when we push ourselves out of them, try to stay in one vibe too long or allow ourselves to get pulled into another's.

*Universe, today I have my own vibe.*

Dear Universe,

Today I ask that you help me to remember: *We have to fight the voices within us that tell us we should be ashamed for wanting to be happy.*

Tell them to be quiet! Tell them they don't know what they are talking about. Tell them they've got the wrong number. Tell them whatever you need to – but make sure you let that voice inside your head know that it is wrong!

It is wrong to tell you that you don't deserve to be happy. It is wrong to tell you that you have to live your life in service to others, to the detriment of yourself.

Tell that voice to shut it up! Tell that voice you don't want to hear it and you ain't gonna have it! Tell that voice that you are worthy of every little bit of happiness and that you ain't gonna be ashamed, sorry or apologetic about it!

*Universe, today I have me some happy.*

Dear Universe,

Today *I will stop talking s\*it about sex.*

Stop it.

Stop blaming sex. Stop blaming sex for your lack of boundaries. Stop blaming sex for your partner leaving you. Stop blaming sex for you not having a partner. It's not sex's fault.

Stop shaming sex. Stop talking bad about sex. Stop putting sex down.

Sex is not bad. Sex is how you got here. Sex is how life gets here. Sex is about pleasure. Sex is about sensuality and, yes, sometimes sex is about love. *But sex doesn't need to be about love to be okay.*

Fact is, a lot of people blame sex for things that are not sex's responsibility. A lot of people blame sex for things that come out of social stigma, silence, dishonesty, or lack of self-care. A lot of people blame sex for their own choices that they are afraid to be accountable for. A lot of people blame sex because of the way others have used sex against them.

But sex has nothing to do with that. Sex is what it has always been – a sensual experience to be celebrated and not shamed. It is a tool that can be used to affirm our bodies, enrich our lives, or recycle our rage and contribute to our confusion. Sex is what is. Don't let others define sex for you by how they use it. Define it by how you will use it for yourself.

*Universe, today I define sex on my own terms.*

Dear Universe,

Today I ask that you *help me remember magic.*

Look around you. You live on a giant rock that floats in the sky. Look above. The bright yellow star that shines in the sky makes your life possible.

Now just consider: That star holds an entire group of rocks together in a circle. That cosmic circle is made of stardust and bits, from which you are composed and from which, when you perish, you will return.

So um …. what was that you were saying about not believing in magic? What were you saying about not believing in miracles?

Whatever your doubts, surely you must be mistaken. Because if you, my stardust friend, are possible then I am pretty sure whatever acts, great or small, you are attempting pale in comparison to the magic and miracles that it took to get you here in the first place.

*Universe, today I remember I am the magic needed to make it happen.*

## A MESSAGE FROM THE UNIVERSE:

There are some spiritual teachers who will tell you that abundance has nothing to do with *institutions*. They will tell you that abundance stems only from the interior. They will say that any "lack" in your life is always a reflection of you.

This perspective is only one part of the equation.

Institutions, policies and procedures also work to block prosperity.

They can block prosperity through laws that keep people disadvantaged. They can block prosperity by designing systems that do not *distribute income evenly.*

In order for us as a world to end economic inequality, we have to do both the inner work in our hearts, and the outer work in our societies. Until prosperity is present in both realities, poverty and lack will always persevere.

*Universe, today I realize: lack of abundance is internal and institutional.*

Dear Universe,

Today I ask that you help me to understand: *It takes a village to heal a child.*

Our children did not get their wounds alone. They were created by the actions of our family, our communities and our world. They were created by the things we chose to believe in, the causes we chose to champion and the despair we chose to neglect.

We didn't get them from individuals and we cannot heal them operating as individuals. This healing work is communal. It needs to be present in the schools and in the media; in the home and at the playground.

It needs to be present along with the ongoing work that the village must do to *heal itself.*

Healing our children means we need to put love in every possible place we can think of. It means we need to rethink, refeel and reconsider any concept that caused us pain. It means we need to reenergize, reestablish and re-up our commitment to wholeness and joy. Until we do, our children, and our own inner children, will continue to suffer from unnecessary pain.

*Universe, today I work to heal with the village.*

Dear Universe,

Today I will realize: *All children contain emotional remnants of their parents.*

Generation to generation, we inherit the unfinished emotional work of those who came before us.

Whatever emotional lessons you struggle with reflect the emotional lessons they struggled with.

You are the legacy of what your parents left behind. You are the graduate school that teaches every class your parents refused to enroll in. You are the fruit that fell from their tree.

Being that you are that fruit, it is important to remember: If the fruit of the tree does not understand the root from which it came, its seeds will continue to produce the *same old wood.*

*Universe, today I remember where I came from and use that as a map to lead me where I want to go.*

Dear Universe,

Today I ask that you help me to *define myself through myself.*

Some people need you to play the "good cop" so that they can go on pretending they are the "bad cop." Some people need you to play the "bad people" so they can go on believing they are the "good people." Others need you to be a "right winger" so that they can be "left." Or they need you to be "conservative" so that they can continue believing they are "liberal." Some people need you to act a certain way because it justifies their behavior.

When your own sense of identity needs someone else to act a certain way in order for you to understand what you are, then you are in big trouble. It means your self-definition is not dependent on you. It means that you can't define yourself through yourself, but only through the lens of another. *It means you may have lost your true identity!*

For today, take some time to consider the identities to which you subscribe. Could your identity exist if it wasn't for the "other" group out there playing the opposite role in your imagination? And if it cannot, what does that say about who you *think* you are?

*Universe, today I define myself through myself and not through another.*

Dear Universe,

Today I ask that you help me to realize: *What I go out looking for, I will find.*

What are you looking for in the world? Are you looking to be treated unfairly? Expecting to be done wrong? Are you expecting to be loved? Are you expecting to be valued? Whatever it is that you are expecting, you can guarantee that nine times out of ten you are going to find it! And even sometimes when you haven't found it, you'll make up a narrative in your mind so that it looks like you've found it – even when that isn't it!

It doesn't mean that some of your ideas about the world aren't accurate. It does mean that some of your ideas might need to be *reconsidered.* Because if the things you are expecting out in the world are bringing you misery and pain, you may be helping them come into being, by expecting them everywhere that you go!

*Universe, today I leave my expectations of pain in the past where they belong.*

Dear Universe:

_____

_____

_____

_____

_____

_____

_____

_____

_____

_____

_____

_____

_____

_____

_____

_____

_____

_____

_____

_____

_____

_____

Dear Universe:

_____

_____

_____

_____

_____

_____

_____

_____

_____

_____

_____

_____

_____

_____

_____

_____

_____

_____

_____

_____

CPSIA information can be obtained
at www.ICGtesting.com
Printed in the USA
BVOW08s0929130418
513212BV00001B/4/P